POPCORN PARK ZOO

A HAVEN WITH A HEART

by Wendy Pfeffer
Photographs by J. Gerard Smith

JULIAN MESSNER

This book is for my three Little Loves:
Andrew, Timothy, and Jaime.

The author wishes to acknowledge and thank the staff at Popcorn
Park Zoo, especially John who spent hours recalling stories, answering
questions, and introducing me to the fascinating animals at the zoo. I also want to
thank my husband, Tom; my agent, Renee Cho; my editor, Bonnie Brook;
and The Wednesday Workshoppers for their help and solid support which
made my work a pleasure.

Library of Congress Cataloging-in-Publication Data

Pfeffer, Wendy.
Popcorn Park Zoo: a photo essay / Wendy Pfeffer.
p. cm.
Includes bibliographical references and index.
Summary: Describes Popcorn Park Zoo in New Jersey, which
rescues and cares for animals that are sick, old, abused, or about
to be destroyed.
1. Popcorn Park Zoo—Juvenile literature. [1. Popcorn Park Zoo.
2. Zoos.] I. Title.
QL76.5.U6P44   1992
590′.74′474948—dc20

91-3273
CIP
AC

Art Director: Linda Huber
Designed By Frederick J. Latasa

ISBN 0-671-74589-1 (library) ISBN 0-671-74587-5
(hardcover)

Published by Julian Messner, a division of Silver Burdett
Press, Inc., Simon & Schuster, Inc., Prentice Hall Building,
Englewood Cliffs, NJ 07632.

CONTENTS

INTRODUCTION

Welcome to Popcorn Park Zoo. It's an unusual zoo for unusual animals and the only one of its kind in the United States. Popcorn Park Zoo is home to an assortment of animals that would not stand a chance anywhere else. And a little raccoon named Rigby started it all.

On a family farm chickens scratch in the dirt for food and pigs wallow in the mud. In the jungle tigers prowl the underbrush while monkeys swing through the trees. On the African grasslands a ten-thousand-pound elephant nuzzles its newborn calf. In scrub forests deer romp freely. On a dark country road a family of raccoons, caught in the glow of headlights, scrambles back toward the thicket. Animals live in many different settings, but examples of *all* these animals are found in one place—Popcorn Park Zoo.

Located in the Pine Barrens of New Jersey, it is the only federally licensed* zoo in the United States that accepts animals no one else wants, and is financed solely by contributions. The zoo rescues and cares for animals that are hurt, sick, old, abused, unwanted, or about to be destroyed. At Popcorn Park Zoo they get food, shelter, and medical treatment, plus plenty of popcorn and lots of love—all in daily doses.

But Popcorn Park wasn't always a zoo.

It began as the Ocean County branch of the Associated Humane Societies and was called the Forked River Animal Care Center. The center's purpose was to find homes for cats and dogs. Then one evening things changed.

In June 1977, John Bergmann, manager of the Animal Care Center, and Lee Bernstein, director of the Associated Humane Societies of New Jersey, received a call from a worried woman. She reported that there was a raccoon in her backyard whose foot had been caught in a steel leghold trap.* The woman suspected that the animal had dragged it a long way before the chain on the trap became hooked on her fence. The raccoon was dangling from it by one front foot. The hurt and frightened animal was unable to free itself.

John and Lee carefully removed the raccoon from the trap. Then they realized how infected the damaged leg was. Because there was no veterinarian at the Forked River location at that time, they took the raccoon to the Associated Humane Societies in Newark, New Jersey. The doctor there amputated* a portion of the animal's front foot.

The operation was successful, but now the two men were faced with the problem of what to do with a three-legged raccoon that needed its missing front paw to gather food. They knew that the injured animal could not be released back into the wild.

Raccoons live in trees, so John built a large tree house for the animal in a fenced-in area at the center. In September he brought the raccoon, whom he named Rigby, back to the Forked River shelter. Rigby seemed to adjust well to his new home. He climbed around the tree house and lived comfortably, eating his favorite foods: eggs, chicken, marshmallows, and zoo popcorn. This popcorn is specially made without salt or oils, so Rigby could eat all he wanted. And Popcorn Park Zoo was born.

After Rigby, a groundhog named Cuddles and an injured deer called Bam Bam needed help. John added more cages and had another fence built. As more animals came, more cages and more fences were installed. Today, Popcorn Park Zoo provides a refuge for more than two hundred sick, handicapped, old, abused, or abandoned animals.

John is always on the lookout for ways to provide an environment that will permit the animals to live and behave as they would in the wild. He knows that animals that live freely in an open setting are more content. They behave more like they would in their natural environment. He and Popcorn Park officials are concerned with the quality of life that exists at the zoo. Unlike the empty cemented world of many zoos, Popcorn Park's natural habitats* include evergreen and deciduous* trees, rocks, shrubs, water, and the wonderful feeling of wilderness.

Let's tour the zoo to meet some of its amazing inhabitants. But first let's do what most visitors do and buy a box of the zoo's special popcorn.

CHAPTER 1

FIELD AND FOREST ANIMALS

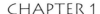s you walk through Popcorn Park Zoo, you may notice that many of the zoo's animals are native to the fields and forests of New Jersey's Pine Barrens. Raccoons, deer, and foxes are a few of the many kinds of wild animals that live here.

Rigby, the zoo's first inhabitant, was not the only casualty of the leghold trap. Other zoo raccoons, named Stitches, Bandit, and Raisin, were also trap victims. Even though they suffered, they were lucky. Skunks, opossums, rabbits, and some raccoons have tried to chew off their own legs to escape. Many have died in these traps. Dogs, cats, birds, squirrels, and many other species* are also victims of this painful device. Even though leghold traps are illegal in New Jersey and in many other states, people still set them to trap raccoons and other fur-bearing animals. Then they kill them and make coats and other types of clothing out of their fur.

Not all of the raccoons at the zoo were casualties of the trap. Rowdy Raccoon had his right foreleg amputated because of a serious infection. When he was sick, he lived up to his name by being loud and unruly. The helpers at the zoo had to catch him and hold him down to give him medicine. When the workers tried to clean his cage, he would climb all over them. When he was getting better, he bounced around in his cage and climbed the walls—upside down.

Several other species of field and forest animals feel at home in the zoo's pineland environment.

Rabbits romp in the sunshine and munch bits of grass, herbs, and clover. In the winter they nibble on bark, twigs, and shrubs. Rabbits at Popcorn Park Zoo once burrowed all over the grounds, as rabbits normally do. But the zoo's rabbits were tunneling under buildings and causing foundations to collapse. In addition, the United States Department of Agriculture, which grants the zoo's license, declared the burrowing unsanitary. This habit had to be stopped. So a large area was fenced in, and hutches to house the rabbits were built about four feet off the ground. Now zoo rabbits do not need to dig a snug nest. Instead they hop contentedly about, then curl up in their cozy hutches.

Ronald Rabbit lives in one of these modern rabbit compounds. Before he came to the zoo, he was a house pet. Bought as an Easter present, he was squeezed, carried around, and dropped on the floor. When the family lost interest in him, they handed Ronald over to the zoo.

What a different life Ronald has from many other Easter pets! When these pets are mishandled they often die within a short time. John likes to remind visitors that if they want a bunny for Easter, "make it a toy bunny."

Not all rabbits at the zoo were Easter presents. Some baby bunnies were taken from their nests in the spring. It's easy to understand why people want them. Bunnies are soft and cuddly, and their floppy ears and sniffing noses are appealing. But they belong in the wild with their mothers.

When people see a fawn by itself, they sometimes think it has been abandoned by its mother. A baby deer, with its big brown eyes and long slim legs, looks so fragile that not everyone can resist taking it home, especially when they believe that the animal is an orphan. However, often the mother is only twenty or thirty feet away but too frightened to go near people. So if you find a baby animal in the woods, it is important to leave it there. If one is really an orphan, call the local police department, animal control warden, humane society, or Popcorn Park Zoo. These places know how to take care of wild animals.

Some well-meaning people adopted a fawn and fed her baby formula. After all, they thought, Steffie *was* a baby. Now Steffie is blind, not because she was allergic to the formula, but possibly because a formula meant for human babies does not have the proper nutrients to help a baby deer to grow.

When she first came to the zoo, Steffie had a difficult time. Any animal has to adjust to new surroundings, but a blind one takes longer. Because loud noises upset Steffie, John talked softly when he approached her so she would not be frightened. The staff tried to anticipate problems that might arise with her. For instance, as John explained, ''We put her in a small pen so she couldn't get up a full head of steam and hurt herself by running into a fence.''

Gradually Steffie learned to walk slowly alongside the fence. But when she left it, she appeared to be afraid to move forward as sighted deer do. Instead, she curved as she walked, almost as if she were walking in circles. Most blind deer do this and then enlarge the circles as they move.

Another blind deer, Wonder Boy, had become separated from his mother during a heavy storm. When he was found deep in the woods, he was frightened and was walking in circles with his head up high, his ears alert. Sounds helped him to know what was happening around him.

After living at the zoo for a while, Wonder Boy got loose. John tracked the blind deer by following his curved trail for three days. When John found Wonder Boy, the deer was only a quarter of a mile away from the zoo.

Steffie and Wonder Boy soon learned the zoo layout and the daily routine so well that it was difficult to tell they were blind. Deer at Popcorn Park Zoo roam freely in their natural habitat. They browse* in natural surroundings, eating a little, napping a bit, then nibbling. They eat, nap, and nibble throughout the day.

When the zoo deer run, the white underside of their tail shows. It's easy to see why they are called white-tailed deer. In summer their reddish brown coloring camouflages* them. In winter they turn grayish brown to match their cold, gray surroundings. The fawns are marked with white dots that look like bits of sunlight. Fawns are odorless, too. These traits make them almost invisible to wild dogs and other enemies.

One year the zoo contained eight deer that romped through the natural scrub forest or browsed contentedly on the forest floor. The next year the zoo took in nineteen more. Many of the deer had been injured by hunters with bad aim. Some deer became brain-damaged. Others hop around on three legs.

Despite their bad experiences with humans, most Popcorn Park deer are comfortable around people. They wander right up to visitors, sometimes nudging them or pulling on their shirts. These beautiful animals stretch out their slender necks and lick the faces of the children who visit them. John hopes this will make a lasting impression on the children. He believes it will help them care about what happens to deer. ''I have faith,'' he said, ''that when these children grow up, they won't be as likely to pick up a gun and shoot.''

Some deer are friendly toward people. Some are shy. All deer are beautiful creatures that usually live in forests and fields.

Whenever a field or forest is bulldozed to build homes or a shopping center, the animals must find a new food chain, water supply, and shelter. They are scared and confused, and often there is no place to go. Deer and other wildlife at Popcorn Park Zoo are spared this distress.

Another field and forest resident of the zoo is Foxy Loxy. This red fox was an orphan that the zoo rescued when he was just a baby, or kit. A fox kit is completely dependent on its mother for food and protection for the first few months. Both parents usually watch over newborn kits. In Foxy Loxy's case, neither parent was around. The baby was nursed by a zoo staff member at her home until he was old enough to go to Popcorn Park Zoo. There he is safe. No hunter can shoot him. No trapper can lure him. And he will never go hungry. Foxy Loxy enjoys eating turkey and loves ice cream—his favorite is caramel nut.

Despite the love, care, and plates of ice cream the animals get at Popcorn Park or any zoo, nothing can take the place of their natural homes in the wild. That is why many staff members are trained to rehabilitate animals and return them to the wild as soon as they can exist on their own.

Now let's see more of those animals who *don't* have that choice.

CHAPTER 2

FARM ANIMALS

nother common sight at the zoo are farm animals. If you look around Popcorn Park Zoo, you might think you are at Popcorn Park Farm. Even though there are many farms in the area, farm animals come to the zoo from all over the country.

Many of the animals are ordinary farm animals in one respect, but extraordinary in another. Each animal is a survivor and could tell a special story if only it could talk. Because of the dedication of John and the other zoo personnel and the excellent care they provide, most of the animals' sad stories have happy endings.

One of the zoo's most unusual creatures was Marlboro the goat. Late one evening zoo officials received a phone call from the police. They told of strange happenings in the woods outside a nearby town.

Lee Bernstein and a helper drove over dark bumpy roads to an isolated clearing in the trees. They saw a makeshift altar and realized that a bizarre religious ceremony had taken place earlier that evening. Exploring deeper into the woods, they found a goat. He was bleeding and barely alive. His neck had been slashed. "And he was only a little guy," Lee said.

The men lifted the limp animal into the truck.

Back at the zoo more than one hundred stitches were needed to close the wound. The neck muscles were so badly damaged that it took six months of loving care for Marlboro to recover.

While the goat healed, he moved with his head down. Even when he recovered, he never held his misshapen neck upright. Zoo visitors often asked, "What is that animal? Is it some kind of donkey?" He may not have looked like a goat, but in his own way he was special.

Every day, a half hour before the zoo opened, this outgoing, friendly goat went to the zoo gate and waited for the first visitors. He greeted people by nudging them with one leg and begged for a handful of popcorn. Then he acted as their personal tour guide, leading a whole family around the park until they left. After they had gone, Marlboro would go back to the gate to greet, nudge, and escort another group of visitors. He did this until closing time every day.

How amazing it was that he loved and trusted people. After all, it was a human being who had hurt him. But this love and trust helped him to make thousands of friends for Popcorn Park during his eleven-year stay there. After he died many people missed him.

"**M**arlboro is really what Popcorn Park Zoo is all about," John said. "We get animals in dire need, and we try to help them live some kind of normal life."

Since farms are common in the area, the zoo has become a haven to other goats, too. They eat grass, which they quickly swallow and then store in a special stomach to chew later as cud. They also like alfalfa, vegetables, and plants. And when the zoo used old Christmas trees as a windshield, the goats ate them, too. Even though goats have a reputation for eating almost anything, they really don't. And they don't eat tin cans, either. They just lick them to taste the glue on the labels.

When a gardener found a billy goat munching her gardenias for breakfast, she complained. The goat was caught by a policeman, put in the back seat of the patrol car, and taken to headquarters. Then the police called Popcorn Park Zoo. John brought the goat to the zoo and named him Gardenia. He seems to be happy—even though gardenias are not served for breakfast.

Dorinda and Holly arrived at the zoo at the same time. Holly is a short, overweight Sicilian donkey with a placid personality. Dorinda, a goat, was much smaller and had a skinny ragged beard. Dorinda was shy and followed Holly everywhere. Their young owner cared for them as part of her 4-H project. When she grew up and went away to college, she couldn't take care of them anymore, but she wanted them to go to a good home. They did. At Popcorn Park Zoo they spent their days sunning themselves and going everywhere together. When Dorinda died, Holly was depressed, but later she made some new friends at the zoo.

In addition to goats, the zoo has other farmyard animals. There are sheep, pigs, chickens, geese, horses, ponies, and a bull named Ferdinand.

Sheep are one of humans' most important tamed animals because they give us wool to make warm clothing. A sheep gave the residents of Bridgewater, New Jersey, some excitement as well.

One brisk autumn day a stray sheep with an auction tag on her ear was spotted wandering along a major highway. Local animal control officers were called, but for several weeks they could not catch her.

The female sheep, or ewe, romped on and off the busy road. She had plenty of grass and wild apples to eat, and a small stream for water. But the officers were worried. She could easily be hit by a car or truck.

Finally, the officers called John. He brought a male sheep, or ram, named Wooley Nelson to attract her. He had a circular fence built and put Wooley inside it, tied to a stake. At one end was an opening where the ewe could enter. Four hours went by before she finally joined Wooley. At Popcorn Park Zoo she was named Bridget after the town where she had her adventure.

Another animal rescued from a major highway was a three-month-old piglet. She probably escaped from a farm and made her way to the parkway. There she enjoyed herself. She rooted* with her snout in the

dirt. She wallowed in the water that ran under the parkway. And she stayed clear of the people called in to snare her.

Several motorists called John. He came out three times before he found the pig. When he finally spotted her, he clapped his hands loudly to scare her so that he could see where she ran. Then he spread corn on the ground, hid under a nearby bridge, and waited.

With her keen sense of smell, the pig was soon tempted by the treat. When she came close, John reached out and grabbed her by the ear. She squealed frantically. "You'd think I was killing her," John said. To get a good grip on her, John wrapped the pig in a blanket. Named the Parkway Porker, she now roots and wallows in her own pen at Popcorn Park Zoo, beside her "pen pal" Arnette.

Vietnamese pot-bellied pigs are becoming very popular as pets. Dudley Morris is one of these. He's small and gentle, with a little straight tail that wags all the time. His owners bought him for $1,000. They lived on the twentieth floor of an apartment building.

Dudley did what all pigs do naturally. He grunted when he "talked" and squealed when he was hurt or excited. And as all pigs do instinctively, he rooted. But when he did this, he would rearrange the furniture, pull electrical plugs from their outlets, and snuggle his snout into expensive rugs.

His owners soon realized that a pig, no matter how small it would always be, was not suited for apartment life. After two weeks they gave Dudley Morris up. But their loss was Popcorn Park Zoo's gain.

Chickens peck and scratch in the dirt all over the park. One defenseless hen was the victim of senseless cruelty. She was stuffed into a mailbox and the lid was snapped shut. Someone discovered the injured animal and sent her to Popcorn Park Zoo. She was named Zip because she was the only chicken known to have reached its destination without a stamp or a zip code.

The SPCA* regularly calls the police to break up cockfights. Sugar Ray Rooster is one of several fighting cocks they saved. In a cockfight two specially-bred roosters battle each other in a fight to the death. This is illegal in the United States, but it is often carried on secretly. Sugar Ray was bred for speed, courage, physical strength, and a killer instinct. Now he engages in peaceful pecking.

Heckel and Jeckel are two white Chinese geese that probably escaped from a nearby family farm. They patrol the zoo like watchdogs and heckle new arrivals.

Red and Star were two gentle ponies that had been used in a traveling circus merry-go-round. Even though both ponies had painful saddle sores, the circus didn't attend to them. The circus would let children ride these animals without giving them a rest. The SPCA was concerned and brought them to the zoo. At Popcorn Park Zoo, Red and Star were never mistreated again. They spent the rest of their days contentedly roaming the fields and deciding what to eat next—carrots, apples, or oatmeal cookies.

Ferdinand was a baby bull that lived on a farm resort. Young animals were kept there just to provide a farmlike atmosphere for the guests. At the end of each summer the animals were slaughtered.

One of the guests had become devoted to Ferdinand. When she learned that the bull was going to the slaughterhouse, she bought him for $125 and brought him to Popcorn Park Zoo.

Ferdinand begs for zoo popcorn from the visitors by sticking his head over the fence and rolling out his tongue. When he gets some popcorn, he curls up his tongue and eats the treat. Then he rolls out his tongue again for more popcorn. Some visitors spend hours watching him.

The sound of hens cackling, roosters crowing, horses whinnying, sheep bleating, and pigs squealing is music to the ears of the zoo's visitors. But they are just as happy listening to the screeching peacocks, growling bears, trumpeting elephant, and the roaring of Lacey the lion. Let's go visit Lacey next.

BIG GAME AND EXOTIC ANIMALS

 male lion was Popcorn Park Zoo's first large exotic* animal. His name is Lacey, after the township in which the zoo is located. Lions are one of the largest members of the cat family. They usually have powerful bodies. Lacey has a strong body now, but there was a time when he did not.

Lacey was once part of a magician's act. Because he was not properly fed, he became sick with rickets* and developed other health problems. His veterinarian's receptionist was a volunteer for the Salem County Humane Society of Ohio. She wanted Lacey to have a better home and told the humane society about him.

When the lion's medical bills became too high, the magician sold him to the society. They agreed to pay the medical bills in exchange for the lion.

The humane society kept Lacey for a year while they tried to find a proper home for him. But no zoo or safari park wanted a declawed* male lion that couldn't defend itself.

The society finally considered putting him to sleep unless a permanent home could be found. Luckily they read an article about Popcorn Park Zoo and called them. That phone call saved Lacey's life.

Today Lacey looks strong and regal with his large head and long bushy mane. When he lifts his head and roars, he can rightly be called the "King of Beasts." Lions like to be with other lions, and in the wild they always travel in prides.* Lacey seems to be content now, living with Popcorn Park's lioness, Sheena.

Sheena was once a cuddly house pet. After a while she did what cats naturally do. She grew up. She got so big the town officials pressured Sheena's owner to get rid of her. A tamed lioness cannot survive in the wild. So the owner called Popcorn Park Zoo and asked them to take her. Placing an adult cat in an established pride is difficult because it is hard for the new lion to be accepted.

Both Lacey and Sheena were raised without knowing another lion. When Sheena arrived at the zoo, her small temporary pen was placed next to Lacey's outdoor area. They got to know each other gradually, first by sight, then by scent. After two months her solid door was replaced by bars so they could be nose to nose. After three months Sheena was moved to Lacey's compound.* They have had no problems adapting to life together.

On warm days Lacey and Sheena like to lie in the shade. Because lions breed often in captivity, Lacey has been altered* so that Popcorn Park Zoo does not contribute to the overpopulation of lions in captivity.

One look at Bunkie and it's easy to understand how anyone might consider adopting a lion cub. Bunkie arrived at Popcorn Park Zoo on Super Bowl Sunday, eight weeks old, cute, cuddly, and as playful as a kitten.

He was not playful, however, when a veterinarian named Dr. Paluch first examined him. Bunkie was four weeks old, skinny, and almost dead. An unidentified man had left the sick cub with Dr. Paluch and never came back for him.

The vet took Bunkie home and nursed him. At eight weeks of age Bunkie weighed nine pounds and was strong enough to be turned over to the zoo.

Even though Bunkie was completely helpless at birth, by two years of age Bunkie will be an adult. His fluffy spotted baby fur will be sleek and golden brown and his plump body will have stretched out long and lean. His mane will grow longer, thicker and quite dark by the time he is five.

Bunkie may live to be twenty or thirty years old. In the wild a lion is lucky to reach the age of seventeen. But, at the zoo Bunkie is well fed and doesn't face the dangers lions must overcome in nature.

A tiger is usually one of a zoo's most fearsome residents. Tina, Popcorn Park Zoo's tiger, is not to be feared. John says she's a "love." But this wasn't always true. She was once in the side show of a traveling circus. She lived, ate, and slept in a stark, cramped cage housed in a trailer. A black bear, hyena, leopard, and two crab-eating macaque monkeys also lived in the trailer.

Late one night the circus caravan was traveling along the Garden State Parkway in New Jersey and the old trailer broke down. As the driver tried to fix the trailer, a state trooper arrived. At first he thought the trailer contained only tents and circus equipment. When he discovered that animals were inside, he had the trailer towed to a garage.

A day passed. No one came for Tina or the other animals. Two days passed. Popcorn Park Zoo was called to feed and water the abandoned animals. The SPCA signed complaints against the owners for neglect. The trailer was towed to the zoo to make it easier to care for the animals. The leopard's owner came for his animal but no one claimed the others, so Popcorn Park Zoo kept them all.

In the trailer Tina was upset and growled at everyone. She was nervous her first night at the zoo. John stayed with her and reassured her just as he might stay with a sick or hurt animal. Tina was upset during her first thunderstorm at the zoo, so John stayed with her that night as well. That was more than four years ago. Now Tina purrs and comes to John when he calls her.

While in the circus trailer, Tina had only known her small cage and its hard steel floor. At the zoo when she first felt sand and pine needles beneath her feet, she tried to shake them off. She walked on the cement curbing that held the fencing in place until she became accustomed to sand between her toes and pine needles under her feet.

Unlike most cats, Tina loves to swim. On hot days only her nostrils and ears poke above the water. She now lives a happy, contented life.

Another large member of the cat family residing in the zoo is Cindy Lou, a cougar. Cougars are also called mountain lions because early settlers in our country incorrectly thought all cougars were female lions.

Cindy Lou was once a pet living in Iowa. She survived a car crash in which her owner died. The owner had had her declawed to make her acceptable as a house pet. But because of that, Cindy Lou would never again be able to fend for herself.

When Cindy Lou calls out with her soft whistle, John whistles back. Not only do the two of them communicate, they play together. The only time Cindy Lou growls is when she and Tasha, another cougar, are eating. Food is serious business to cougars.

Still another cat is Rajah the bobcat, a type of North American wildcat. Wild animals are not meant to be kept indoors, and some states have laws against people doing this. Rajah was from Missouri, where it is legal to keep pet bobcats. When his owner moved to New Jersey, he found it was illegal to keep wild animals as pets. Rajah had been declawed, his

canine* teeth filed, and the back teeth rounded off. He could not have survived in the wild. Rajah had been fed cat food, which did not have enough nutrition for him to thrive. But three months after he arrived at Popcorn Park Zoo, Rajah had gained fifteen pounds.

Bird Reynolds, a black crow, lives in the cage next to Rajah. The crow keeps a sharp lookout over the bobcat's activities. At the same time the bobcat stares at the crow. Bird Reynolds plays an important role in the bobcat's life at the zoo.

One visitor felt that it was cruel to put the crow next to Rajah since the bobcat was frustrated at not being able to reach him. However, John thinks that this arrangement stimulates the bobcat's mind. Rajah stalks the crow just as he would have stalked prey in the wild.

It's a game for both the cat and the bird. When Bird Reynolds sees Rajah stalking, he flies around the cage as if to get away. This makes Bird Reynolds stay alert and exercises his muscles, too.

Another feathered creature—who is heard more than seen—is Jocko, a loud-mouthed blue-fronted Amazon parrot. He is a brilliantly colored bird and can talk. He was rejected by his owners after his piercing screeches and constant loud, harsh voice became the complaint of the neighborhood.

Jocko lives in John's office and is a one-person bird. Jocko sits on John's desk, nuzzling him and demanding all of his attention. When John's assistants come to the door, jealous Jocko swoops down and scares them. He screeches when visitors stay too long.

"**H**e's just like a child when I'm on the phone," John said, "flying about and screaming. As soon as I hang up, Jocko quiets down." This is all typical parrot behavior. In the wild Jocko would be just as protective toward his mate.

Four bears—two females and two males—live at the zoo. The males and females are separated by an electric fence so they won't fight. There is also a dry moat around the outside of the compound to keep them away from visitors.

Osa and Ursala are black bears. When they were cubs, these sisters were displayed in a roadside zoo to attract tourists. When they got too big to be cute, their owner did not care for them properly. He beat them with shovels and did not feed them enough or give them proper medical care. Bears usually have shaggy fur, but their coats were ragged. Luckily they were rescued by an animal lover who gave them food and shelter. But when she ran out of funds and space, the woman offered them to the Associated Humane Societies. Popcorn Park Zoo welcomed its first big native animals.

Osa and Ursala lumber around in a comfortable compound, complete with a waterfall and a swimming pool in which they love to splash and play. They have rocks and trees to climb and hide behind, as well as old tires and bowling balls to play with. (Regular rubber balls would be destroyed in a short time.) For fun the bears roll around and beg for zoo popcorn. Their favorite treats are corn-on-the-cob, honey, apples, and watermelon.

Smokey Bear was in the traveling circus with Tina the tiger. He spends most of his day wrestling with Bubba Bear. They seem to enjoy getting into mischief and will sit up so people will give them popcorn. They share the outdoor compound during the day and a den at night.

Bubba was a pet bear cub from New York. After keeping him for a few days, the owner found that the cub was growing at a rapid pace. When he realized that he could neither keep Bubba nor return this tiny cub to the wild, the owner called the Associated Humane Societies.

On April Fool's Day, Bubba was ten weeks old and living in John's house. He fed Bubba from a baby bottle. John related, "If I paused for only a second offering Bubba that bottle, he became angry and upset. He tried to bite and scratch me. And ten-week-old bears do have teeth."

One day a severe thunderstorm struck. Bubba ran frantically around and hid in the kitchen. Later, when Bubba was moved into the compound, another thunderstorm hit. Bubba ran hysterically around and then climbed a tree for safety. John knew this was the worst place for Bubba to be. He yelled, and after a while Bubba worked his way down and bolted into his den. He still doesn't like thunderstorms.

At ten weeks Bubba weighed eight pounds. John's family wheeled him around in a wheelbarrow. He'd never fit now: Bubba weighs about five hundred pounds and is seven feet tall. Even though Bubba has a large, heavy body with short legs he can easily climb trees. He has no fear of humans and wants to play with them even though he's too big for this. Bubba can roll over and sit down on his haunches to beg for popcorn, stretching out his forepaws in an almost human way.

Louie the llama was three months old and blind when he was given to the zoo. Louie's blindness was caused by cataracts* in both eyes. He was not very friendly toward people when he arrived at the zoo, because he could not see them.

One day John took Louie for a ride in the van. After a while he gently carried Louie, who weighed about seventy-five pounds, into the office of Dr. Clinton, a veterinary ophthalmologist.* The doctor said that surgery was Louie's only chance to see.

John helped place Louie on the operating table. He watched as the llama was given a general anesthetic.* This was administered through a long tube that was passed down Louie's throat. Louie felt no pain.

The doctor removed the cloudy lens from one eye. He did not need to put in an artificial lens as he would with humans. When Louie came out of the anesthetic, John lifted him off the table and carried him outside for some fresh air.

The night after the surgery John went to see Louie. The llama flinched when John's hand moved near him. Life would never be the same for Louie again. He could see!

Now Louie the llama lives contentedly at the zoo—not far from some chattering monkeys!

CHAPTER 4

MONKEYS, MONKEYS, MONKEYS

The Popcorn Park Zoo monkeys play tricks, tease each other, and badger the visitors. Some monkeys squirt water from their mouths at the onlookers, then laugh out loud. They amuse themselves by imitating the visitors and trying to catch the popcorn thrown to them. Besides swinging on a trapeze—using both their arms and their tails— the monkeys can slide down a pole. Their long, strong tails are almost as useful as another pair of hands. Often they use their feet like hands because their toes are like thumbs and fingers. They perform like circus acrobats.

Cappy, a capuchin monkey native to Central and South America, is the oldest in-habitant in the zoo. Someone tied his cage by the doorstep outside the Associated Humane Societies in Newark in May 1977.

Cappy has personality plus. When he sees John, he screeches until John goes over and says hello. Cappy also screams when he is angry or alarmed. When he wants to complain, he makes low sad sounds. Cappy seems to be able to communicate easily. He makes gestures and sounds to let John know what he wants. John says that animals, especially monkeys, have a keen perception of people's body language. Cappy responds readily to kindness. He is a friendly, mischievous comic who shares his cage with a female capuchin monkey, Pepe.

Capuchins are more intelligent than most animals. John realizes this and hangs maze-shaped feeders filled with peanuts outside their cages. Cappy and Pepe can each put a hand in their feeder but can't easily get the food. They have to move the peanut to a certain spot in their maze before it will come out. These monkeys spend hours outsmarting the maze and eating the peanuts.

Besides popcorn and peanuts, Cappy and Pepe enjoy grapes, cookies, raisins, oranges, and melon, as well as commercial monkey chow. They look as if they are deep in thought while munching their food. The monkeys eat throughout the day but are fed each morning and evening.

Clementine, a macaque, or short-tailed, monkey found in Asia, Japan, and Africa, was a five-year-old living at the Prospect Park Zoo in Brooklyn, New York. A group of teenage vandals broke into the zoo and hosed her down with scalding water. Clementine suffered burns over 50 percent of her body. Dr. Adams, the zoo veterinarian, took her home and tenderly cared for her. She lost quite a bit of her reddish brown hair, and it will never grow back. Zoo officials decided that she should be relocated and start a new life.

Despite her bad experience, Clementine is loving, friendly, and responsive to people. She will sit in their laps and accept them in a friendly way. Now she has become a companion to Bobo, another macaque monkey. They communicate with each other and clean each other by picking off the dirt from their bodies. These monkeys enjoy their life at the zoo. Zoologists believe that captive monkeys are happier and healthier when they live outside, so the zoo monkeys live in outdoor cages when the weather is nice. Clementine and Bobo are rather quiet and inactive because they are old. But they're not too old to enjoy mealtimes together, especially when cantaloupes and oranges are on the menu.

Let's leave these entertaining monkeys and head over to see Sonny the African elephant, an endangered species. African elephants were once very common but are now rare.

SONNY THE ELEPHANT

Six-thousand-pound Sonny proved he'd be a handful even before his feet touched the ground at Popcorn Park Zoo. He refused to get out of the forty-five-foot-long tractor-trailer that had hauled him from New Mexico.

John took one look at the elephant and said, "This is going to be a real experience, pal, for both of us." It's no easy matter to contend with one of the biggest animals that live on earth.

To get Sonny out of the trailer, John put a rope around Sonny's leg and he and his crew pulled a little. Then Sonny pulled, then the crew, then Sonny. It took two and a half hours for John and his helpers to get the elephant off the trailer and into his quarters. Immediately John suspected that Sonny would be too stubborn to train. And he was right.

At the New Mexico Zoo, Sonny not only outgrew his quarters, he ripped the place apart. He literally tore his compound down. He picked up the telephone poles that his pen was made of and tossed them around like toothpicks. Once or twice he escaped. The facility wasn't strong enough to hold him, and there wasn't enough for Sonny to do.

The New Mexico Zoo had accepted Sonny as a young elephant. He was shipped there when his herd was culled.* When he grew larger and stronger, the zoo officials decided they couldn't keep Sonny because he was a problem for them. And they couldn't easily find him a new home since most zoos do not want a disfigured animal. Sonny has a tear in his trunk. The zoo people believe that as a baby in Africa, he tangled with a "big cat," perhaps a leopard.

Even with the tear, Sonny can lift and toss a ton of tree trunks or pinch a blade of grass. He can pick up a peanut or a piece of zoo popcorn and put it in his mouth. With his trunk, Sonny drinks, touches, smells, feeds himself, gives himself a shower, makes a loud trumpeting noise, and strips leaves off trees. Sonny's trunk is six feet long and boneless. It is both flexible and strong. If he had to, he could use it to fight enemies, caress his young, or pull a tree out of the ground. People use their hands, nose, and mouth for all the things Sonny does with his trunk. Yet in New Mexico it looked as though the rambunctious thirteen-year-old elephant would have to be put to sleep.

The Friends of Elephants, an animals' rights group in California, decided to rescue Sonny. They called Popcorn Park Zoo officials, who said they would accept him. John, who opens his heart to all animals, not only agreed to take Sonny but spent the first night with him in his new paddock. Neither one slept.

"Animals are excited the first night," John said. "I'd rather be with them than at home worrying about them. I felt if Sonny were going to break something or get into trouble, maybe I could talk him out of it."

When morning came, Sonny tried to escape. "He pushed against everything," John said, "looking for a weak point. When nothing would give, he looked around to see where he was." It took Sonny about three months to settle into the daily routine at the zoo.

Fortunately the zoo has much to keep Sonny busy. He has adapted beautifully to his new surroundings, which include a big yard with a swimming pool. Since elephants have no sweat glands, Sonny must wet himself continually to keep his skin from cracking in the heat. By nature his skin appears baggy and wrinkled and looks as if it doesn't fit.

Sonny also has a scratching post on his grounds. This is a cement tree with an upright branch to scratch his head and a horizontal branch to scratch his belly. Sonny's area is contained by an eight-foot-deep dry moat. If he should tumble in, there are cedar chips to cushion his fall and a stairway so he can climb out. Across the stairway are electric bars so he can't walk down the stairs.

John calls Sonny a typical teenager because he eats all the time. Each day he consumes about two bales of hay, fifty pounds of grain, and thirty pounds of fruits and vegetables, including apples, carrots, and big heads of lettuce. He is seven and a half feet tall and will probably grow to eleven or twelve feet tall. He weighs six thousand pounds now, but someday he will probably be twelve thousand pounds. An elephant is one of the few mammals that continues to grow throughout its lifetime, which for Sonny might be sixty years.